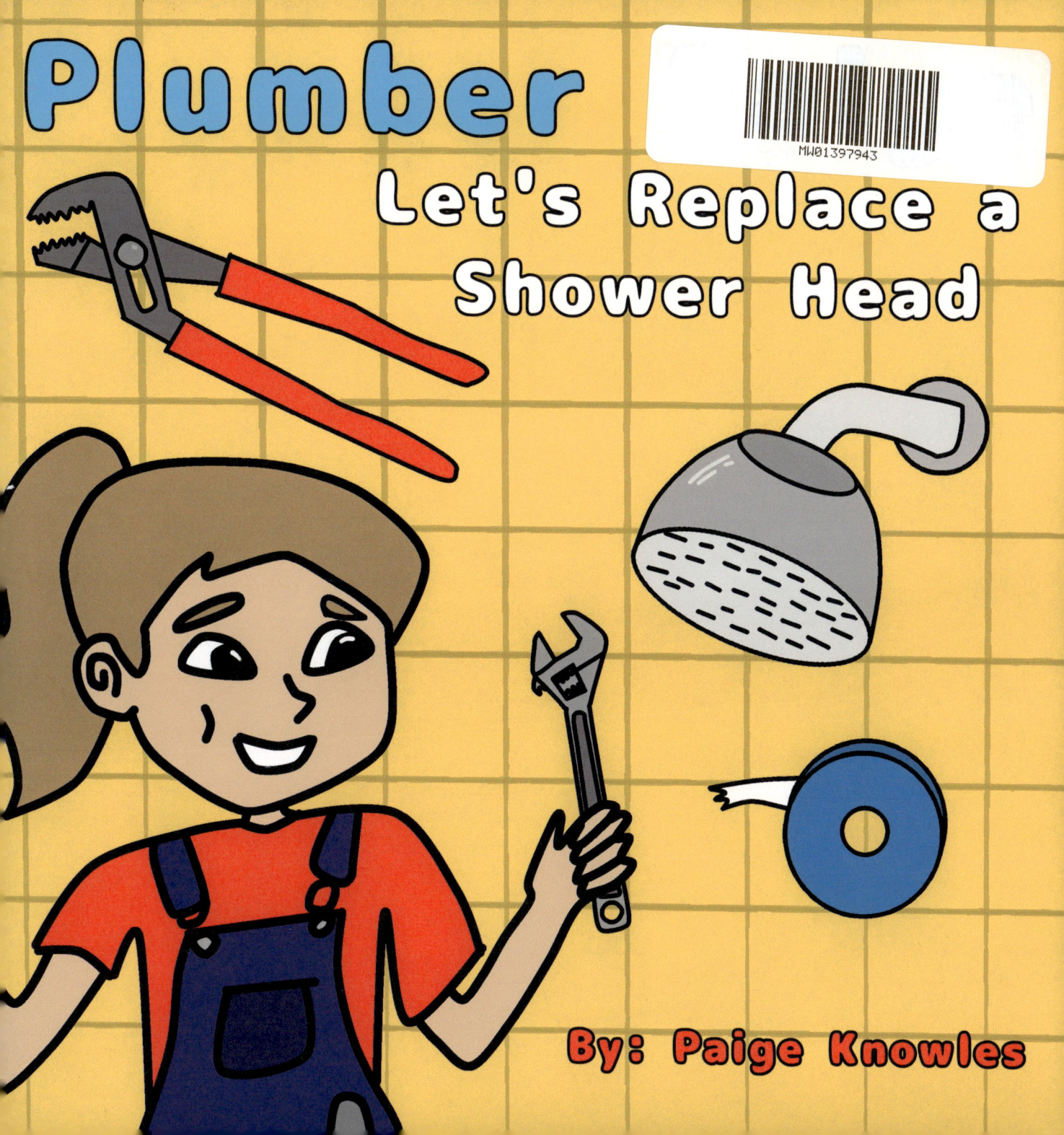

This book is dedicated to:

My parents for encouraging me to believe in myself and do great things!

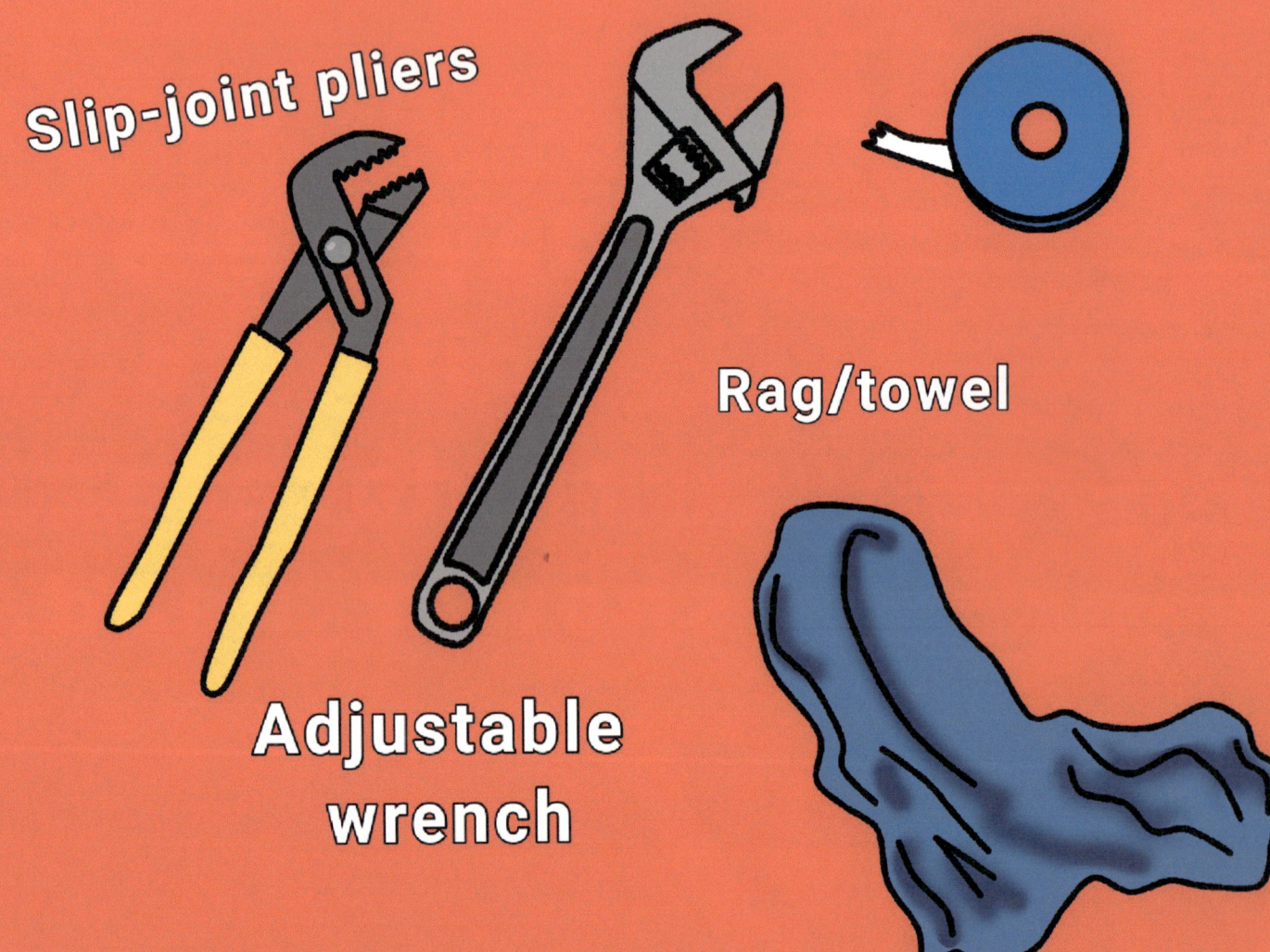

And of course...

The new shower head!

Step three:

Apply 2 to 3 rounds of teflon tape on the threads.

Tip:

Make sure to push the tape into the threads in a clockwise direction.

Step four:

Twist on the new shower head.

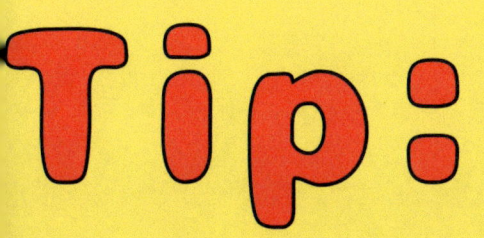

Tip:

Hand tight, turning to the right.

Use a wrench with a towel wrapped around the pipe if it feels loose.

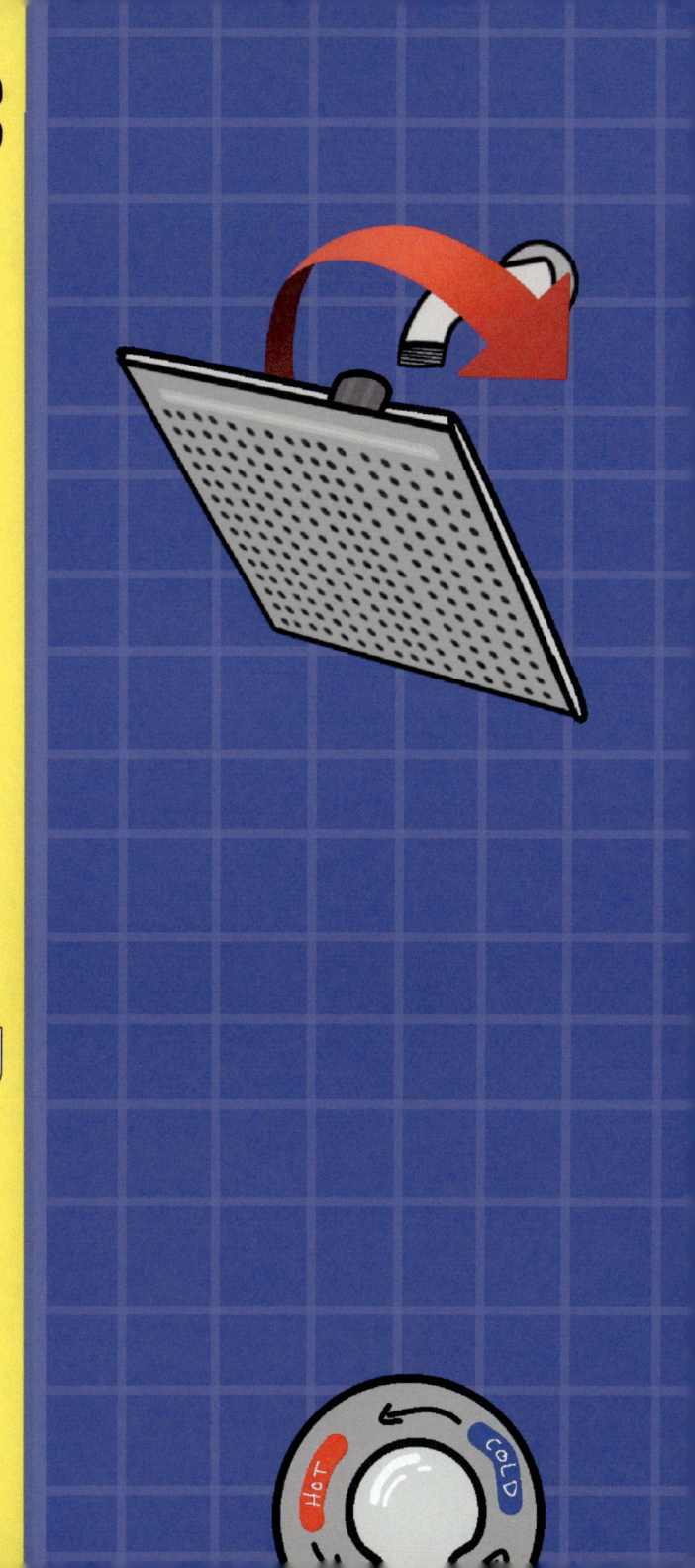

Thanks for coming along with me!

Let's review what we did on the next page.

To replace Mrs. Smith's shower head...

1st: We took off the old shower head.

2nd: Clean off any gunk left on the arm with a rag.

3rd: Press teflon tape into the threads.

4th: Hand tight the new head onto the arm.

5th: Check for leaks.

Lastly: Clean up your work area.

About the Author

Paige Knowles

Paige Knowles is a 2020 high school graduate from the plumbing and heating lab at Lehigh Career and Technical Institute (LCTI). Since graduation she has become determined to be an advocate for the trades. She works closely with Let's Build Construction Camp for Girl's (learn more about them at letsbuildcamp.com). She hopes to start speaking publicly to schools around the world to encourage students to consider a path in the construction industry.

Find out more about Paige and how you can support her mission on her website: plumberpaige.com or find her on social media!

Plumber Paige - YouTube
Instagram - plumber_paige
Paige Knowles - Facebook
Tik Tok - plumber_paige
plumber_paige - Twitter

Made in the USA
Columbia, SC
23 June 2025